Suzuki

VIOLA SCHOOL

Volume 1
Viola Part
Revised Edition

AMPV:1.01

© 2013, 2009, 1981 Dr. Shinichi Suzuki
Sole publisher for the entire world except Japan:
Summy-Birchard, Inc.
Exclusive print rights administered by Alfred Music Publishing Co., Inc.
All rights reserved   Printed in USA

Available in the following formats: Book (0241S), Book & CD Kit (40685), CD (0543)

Book
ISBN-10: 0-87487-241-3
ISBN-13: 978-0-87487-241-5

Book & CD Kit
ISBN-10: 0-7390-9705-9
ISBN-13: 978-0-7390-9705-2

The Suzuki name, logo and wheel device
are trademarks of Dr. Shinichi Suzuki
used under exclusive license by Summy-Birchard, Inc.

This transposition of the SUZUKI VIOLIN SCHOOL makes available to the beginning viola student the carefully structured repertoire of The Suzuki Method®- a method that teaches basic playing skills and develops listening and memorizing ability through the playing of beautiful music.

Regardless of the age of the student, it is hoped that Dr. Suzuki's principles of learning by listening, training the memory, and concentrating on producing a beautiful tone will be observed. Remember that ability develops after a composition has been learned - in the mastering process. The practice suggestions emphasize the need to isolate technical and musical problems, and encourage the teacher to use all the opportunities inherent in the repertoire for orderly growth toward mastery of the instrument.

This volume is also recommended for violinists who wish to become familiar with the viola and reading of the alto clef. For this reason, finger numbers have been kept to a minimum in order that reading will progress by note rather than by finger. The teacher is urged to stress knowledge of names of first-position notes on the viola before note reading progresses to the higher positions.

Many of the solos in this volume are written in the same keys as those in the corresponding SUZUKI CELLO SCHOOL repertoire; also, some solos can be played with the compositions in the SUZUKI VIOLIN SCHOOL.

Doris Preucil

INTRODUCTION

FOR THE STUDENT: This material is part of the worldwide Suzuki Method® of teaching. The companion recording should be used along with this publication. A piano accompaniment book is also available for this material.

FOR THE TEACHER: In order to be an effective Suzuki teacher, ongoing education is encouraged. Each regional Suzuki association provides teacher development for its membership via conferences, institutes, short-term and long-term programs. In order to remain current, you are encouraged to become a member of your regional Suzuki association, and, if not already included, the International Suzuki Association.

FOR THE PARENT: Credentials are essential for any Suzuki teacher you choose. We recommend you ask your teacher for his or her credentials, especially those related to training in the Suzuki Method®. The Suzuki Method® experience should foster a positive relationship among the teacher, parent and child. Choosing the right teacher is of the utmost importance.

In order to obtain more information about the Suzuki Association in your region, please contact:

International Suzuki Association
www.internationalsuzuki.org

CONTENTS

Transcribed for viola and piano by Doris Preucil

Suzuki Viola Method

Principles of Study and Guidance

Four Essential Points for Teachers and Parents

1. The child should listen to the reference recordings every day at home to develop musical sensitivity. Rapid progress depends on this listening.

2. Tonalization, or the production of a beautiful tone, should be stressed in the lesson and at home.

3. Constant attention should be given to accurate intonation, correct posture, and the proper bow hold.

4. Parents and teachers should strive to motivate the child so he will enjoy practicing correctly at home.

Through the experience I have gained in teaching young children for over thirty years, I am thoroughly convinced that musical ability can be fully cultivated in every child if the above four points are faithfully observed.

Musical ability is not an inborn talent but an ability that can be developed. Any child who is properly trained can develop musical ability just as all children develop the ability to speak their mother tongue. For the happiness of children, I hope these four essential points will be carefully observed and put to continual use in the home and studio.

Education for musical sensitivity

Every day, children should listen to the recordings of the music they are currently studying. This listening helps them make rapid progress. It is the most important factor in the development of musical ability. Those children who have not had enough listening will lack musical sensitivity.

Tonalization for beautiful tone

Just as vocalization is studied in vocal music, so I have introduced tonalization into viola study as a new method of education. It has proved to be most effective. Tonalization should always be included at each lesson and should be a part of the daily practice at home.

Group lessons

The adoption of a new kind of group lesson in which more advanced and younger students play together is extremely effective. The students progress remarkably while enjoying the lessons. I recommend that group lessons be held once a week or at least twice a month.

Private lessons to develop ability

A child should not proceed to a new piece simply because he has learned the fingering and bowing of the present one. His ability must be cultivated further as he plays his piece. I would say to the child, "Now that you know the notes, we can start very important work to develop your ability," and then I would proceed to improve his tone, movements, and musical sensitivity.

The following point is also important. When the child can perform piece A satisfactorily and is given a new piece, B, he should not drop A but should practice both A and B at the same time. Continuously reviewing pieces that he knows as new pieces are added will develop his ability to a higher degree.

Mothers and children should always observe the private lessons of other children. Lessons should vary in length according to the needs of the child. Sometimes a child may have a short lesson, stop and watch another child, and then return for more instruction.

Shinichi Suzuki

Stand with feet comfortably apart (approximately the distance of shoulder span). Left foot should be slightly forward; the back must be straight and balanced between both feet. Turn body to the left to align neck of viola with left foot. Do not twist trunk too far around to the left.

Turn head to the left; place the viola between chin and left shoulder. Note the alignment of nose, strings, elbow, and left foot. A foam-rubber pad will keep the viola from slipping and avoid tension in the left shoulder.

Before using the bow, practice holding the viola without the support of the left hand to assure a firm hold without gripping.

The first bow strokes to be used are the *detaché* (smoothly connected) and *staccato* (short notes separated from each other).Careful attention to the motion, clarity of sound, and rhythmic control of these bowings will lay a firm technical foundation.

The beginning student should set the bow at the middle so that the arm forms two sides of a square; the viola and bow form the other two sides. Forearm motion should be used with a relaxed, comfortably-hanging upper arm. A tape marking the middle of the bow is helpful.

The A string posture is fundamental in developing a vertical approach to bowing and should be completely mastered.

Play with a separation between notes (except for repeated 16th notes that develop *detaché*) when first learning the pieces in this volume. This separation gives time to prepare the finger and bow until quicker coordination develops. Later, the material should be reviewed, increasing the smoothness and length of stroke where appropriate.

Further practice suggestions will be found beginning on page 27.

Preparation is vital to all playing. Instill the habit of thinking "mind, finger, bow, play."

The **basic** posture is the A string posture.

Beginner's bow hold. Thumb below frog.

The thumb and the bow make an oblique angle.

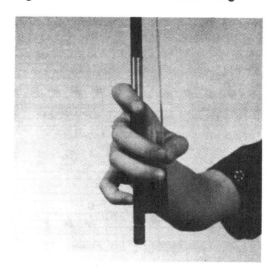

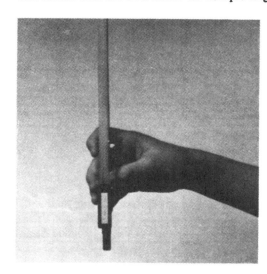

6

Exercises for Proper A-String Posture

The A string posture is fundamental and should be completely mastered.

Set middle of bow on A string.
Use a short stroke.
Keep bow on string between notes.
Sixteenth notes are *detache;* eighth notes are *staccato.*

Exercises for Changing Strings

Change strings quickly here.

Exercises for Quick Placement of Fingers

Place fingers 1, 2, 3 quickly and accurately during rests.

The D Major Scale

Cross to A string.

Prepare fingers 1, 2, 3 on D.
Then cross bow to D. Do not lift bow.

The D Major Scale introduces the first finger-pattern. The beginning pieces employ this pattern — the close 2-3 pattern with a half step between 2 and 3, the interval between the other fingers being a whole step. Develop the mental and aural concept of adding consecutive fingers to ascend stepwise and subtracting consecutive fingers to descend stepwise. Associate the name of each note of the scale with its finger. Also practice this scale with the rhythm patterns taught in "Twinkle, Twinkle, Little Star".

1

Twinkle, Twinkle, Little Star Variations

See Practice Suggestions

Shinichi Suzuki

To play ♪ ♪ stop the bow without pressure after each eighth note.
Bow smoothly and unhurriedly, with a short pause between bow strokes.

Listen for silence during rests.

etc.

Theme

Stop bow without pressure after each note.

2
French Folk Song

Folk Song

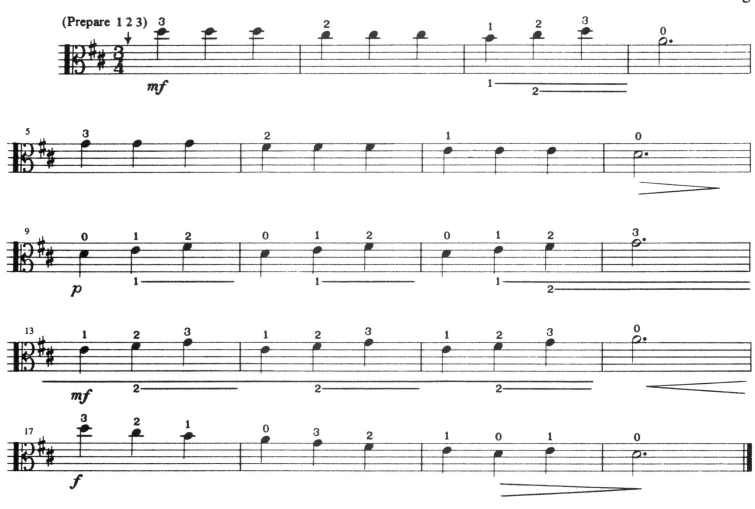

3
Lightly Row

Folk Song

4
Song of the Wind

Folk Song

*Letters in brackets refer to practice suggestions on page 27.

12

5
Go Tell Aunt Rhody

Folk Song

6
O Come, Little Children

Folk Song

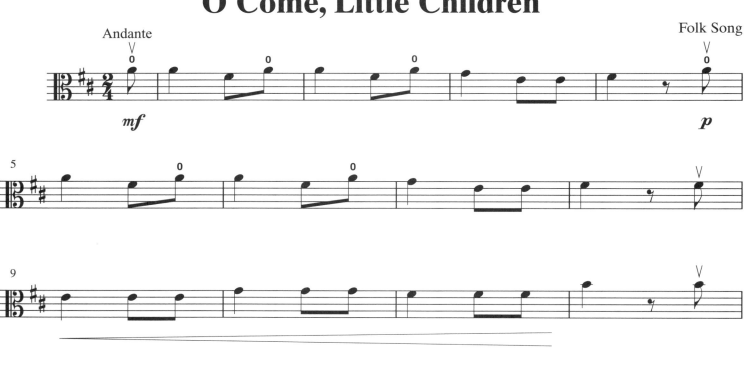

Tonalization

This should be taught at each lesson.
Pluck the open string.
Listen to the sound of the vibrating string.

1

Play the tones with similar resonance with
the bow.

2

3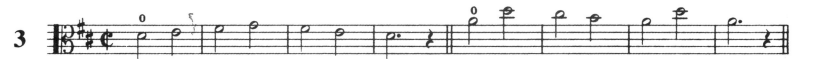

Questions teachers and parents must ask every day:
Are the pupils listening to the reference records at home every day?
Has the tone improved?
Is the intonation correct?
Has the proper playing posture been acquired?
Is the bow being held correctly?

7
May Song

Folk Song

14

Exercises for the 4th Finger

Ease 4th finger reach by moving the left
elbow more to the right.
Hold 1st finger down.

8

Long, Long Ago

T. H. Bayly

9
Allegro

Shinichi Suzuki

Dr. Shinichi Suzuki

Arthur D. Montzka

10
Perpetual Motion

Play at the middle of the bow.
Use a short stroke.
Stop bow after each note to prepare next finger.
Play slowly at first, then gradually increase the tempo.

Shinichi Suzuki

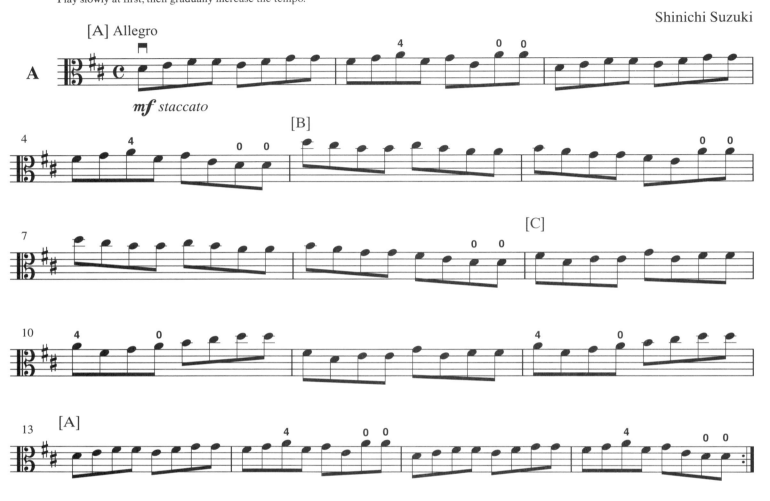

Variation

Feel the two repeated notes as one motion.
Place fingers during rests.

etc.

Tonalization

This should be taught at each lesson.
Pupils should always strive for a more beautiful and resonant tone.

G Major Scale

11
Allegretto

Shinichi Suzuki

12
Andantino

Shinichi Suzuki

The Close 1–2 Pattern

Twinkle, Twinkle, Little Star
(Theme in C Major)

Practice all variations in this key.
Feel the weight of the bow on the C string before playing.
Use less speed in the bow on the lower strings.

C Major Scale
(two octaves)

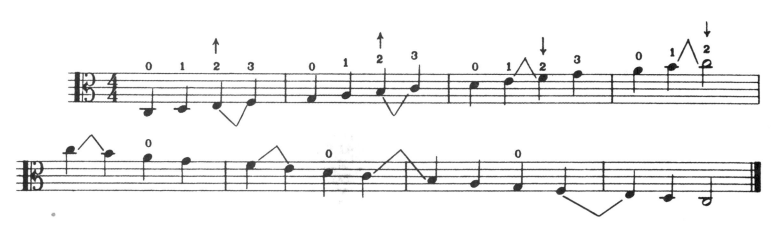

Exercises for Good Intonation
(Diminished Fifths)

13
Bohemian Folk Song

Folk Song

Tonalization

This should be taught at every lesson.

14
Etude

Practice with the same short strokes as Perpetual Motion.
Listen for perfect intonation in high
and low positions of the 2nd finger.

Shinichi Suzuki

Variation

etc.

15
Minuet No. 1

Johann Sebastian Bach

Bowing Patterns

Play these bowing patterns on each note of the C major (two octave) scale.

Circled numbers refer to corresponding numbers in the composition.

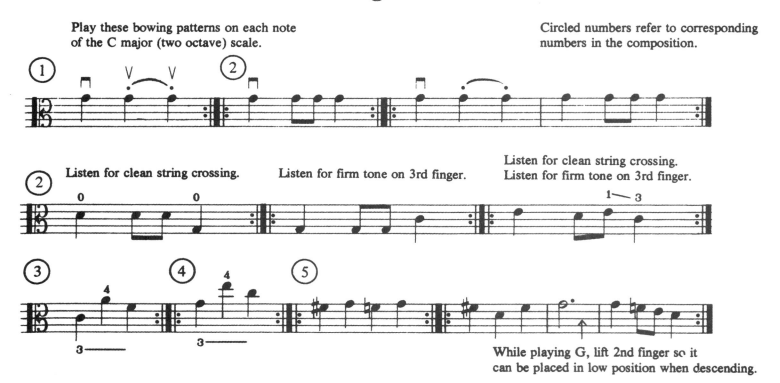

While playing G, lift 2nd finger so it can be placed in low position when descending.

16
Minuet No. 2

Johann Sebastian Bach

*Circled numbers refer to practice suggestions on page 28.

17
Minuet No. 3

Johann Sebastian Bach

*Circled numbers refer to practice suggestions on page 30.

18
The Happy Farmer

Robert Schumann

19
Gavotte

F. J. Gossec

20
Practice Suggestions

"Twinkle, Twinkle, Little Star" Variations

Continue to stop and prepare fingers 1, 2, 3 when descending until a good frame of the hand has been established. The use of tape on the fingerboard to mark correct finger placement is suggested.

Var. B Listen for silence during rests.

Var. C Stop bow only after eighth notes. Use small bow.

Vars. D and E Use small bows. Keep upper arm quiet but relaxed. Set bow at middle, parallel to bridge.

Note that the first and third lines of Twinkle are the same, with a contrasting section in the second line. Form **A B A.**

French Folk Song

Use short strokes with separation between notes. Finger numbers followed by lines indicate holding the fingers down.

Lightly Row

1) Practice the bowing in measure 1 using open strings to achieve matching tone on both strings. Stop bow before crossing. Use short bows. 2) Practice measure 1, placing only the 2nd finger. 3) Listen for the difference between skips of a third and the steps in the scale. 4) Note the form **AA'BA'**, studying the difference between parts **A and A'**.

Song of the Wind   Practice the string crossing and bow lift in measures 3 and 4 on open strings. Hand makes a small, quick circle between two down-bows.

Practice holding 1st finger while lifting and crossing the 3rd finger from D to A string.

Hold silently.

Exercise to strengthen 3rd finger. Do not place 2nd finger.

④ Review the D Major scale, playing all down-bows.

Go Tell Aunt Rhody

1) Most fingerings will not be indicated after this piece to avoid relying on finger numbers in later music reading. 2) As bow control improves, more bow can be used – start at the middle and move further toward tip. Make certain that the bow is kept parallel to the bridge. 3) Note **ABA** form.

O Come, Little Children

1) The most important new technique in this piece is the repeated up-bow that connects each phrase, plus the up-bow beginning. By setting the up-bow at the middle tape, the student will begin to use some of the lower half of the bow. Note that the entire arm is in motion when bowing below the middle. Later, use whole bow with alternating bowing and legato stroke. 2) The skips in this piece provide the opportunity to develop independent fingering. However, it is also important to develop ability to keep fingers down. Adopt this guide for fingering: a) Place only one finger at a time. Fingers either remain down or raise as the next finger falls, depending on the speed and possible repetition of notes.

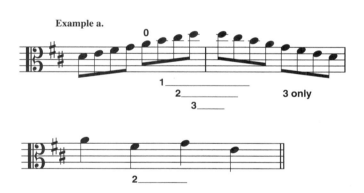

Example a.

b) Go directly from one finger to another ("walking fingers"). Use these principles in reviewing former pieces and in all succeeding learning.

Example b.

Raise 1 when 3 plays, so that it will be ready to fall on A string.

May Song

1) Clap, then play the melodic rhythm of measures 1 and 2 on each note of the D Major scale. 2) Use small bows on dotted quarter notes. 3) Practice the Twinkle Variations on G and D strings.

Exercises for the 4th finger

Adopt this guide for fingering: Use the 4th finger to avoid changing to another string only for that note. In ascending or descending passages, continue to use open strings to check intonation and clarity of tone on fingered notes. In instances of open string usage for musical effect or bow crossing study, the notes will be marked "open" (as in Perpetual Motion).

Long, Long Ago

Use short strokes first. Then use longer, legato strokes with good bow distribution. In measures 9-10, stop the bow and prepare 1st finger on the G string. Cross the string while bow is still, without raising the elbow from the D string posture. Then hold 1st finger until 3 is played; go directly from one finger to another.

Allegro

Use good length and fast speed of bow on quarter notes, with whole arm motion. Keep bow on string at the pause ⌢ , then lift quickly and proceed.

Perpetual Motion

1) The finger action must anticipate the bow stroke. It is important to hear mentally the difference between skips, steps, and repeated notes. 2) Work to develop quick, spring-like action in both placing and lifting fingers. 3) Form **ABCA**. Note the question — answer structure of parts **A** and **B**, differing only in the open string notes (either dominant or tonic). 4) On the repeat, play the Variation. 5) Now play this piece beginning on the G string. The G and C strings, being thicker, should be played with a slightly heavier arm and slower stroke. Avoid the sound of the bow slipping at the beginning of each note.

Allegretto

This piece should be played lightly, without much bow. The eighth notes will alternate from just below to just above the middle.

Andantino

1) Practice ♫ ♪ 𝄾 ♫ ♪ 𝄾 with small, light strokes.
2) The forte section should be played with full bows.

The Close 1-2 Pattern

All the preceding pieces have had C# on the A string and F# on the D string, placing the 2nd finger close to the 3rd. Look back to discover these sharps in the key signatures. If there is no sharp in the key signature or before the note, the note is a natural. C♮ on the A string and F♮ on the D string are both played with the 2nd finger low, touching 1st finger, and leaving a space between the 2nd and 3rd finger. The following pieces will use this new finger pattern on the A and D strings.

(Minuet No. 2)

a.

Keep 1st finger down.
Place 2nd finger close to it on A string.

b.

Take 3rd finger across to G string without lifting 2nd finger until 3rd finger falls. Whenever possible, move directly from one finger to another, as in walking.

c.

Start with 3rd finger only. Hold 1st finger down and place 2nd finger close to it on A string.

Memorize these measures first. Use middle of bow with short strokes. Stop bow between notes, setting new finger before playing.

Cross string rapidly
with 2nd finger.   Hold 2   W.B.   L.H.   W.B.   L.H.   W.B.   U.H.   Save bow.

W.B. - whole bow   U.H. - upper half   L.H. - lower half

Walking Finger Exercises

Bars 12-13

Lift 3rd finger when 4th finger falls.

Practice triplet slowly, then slur.

Feel a steady pulse. Feel triplet lead to second beat.

These exercises prepare the close 3-4 pattern introduced in Minuet No. 2.

slide up

Raise 1st finger during triplet to be ready to fall on D string.

A review of the 3 finger patterns learned.

Pattern 1   Pattern 2   Pattern 3

close   2 - 3   close   1 - 2   close   3 - 4

Practice to achieve a smooth slur across strings.

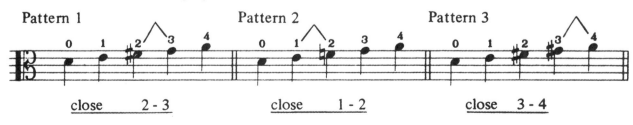

(Minuet No. 3)

Achieve a clear tone with 3rd finger on each string.
Listen for a clear bow release before crossing strings.

① a.

Use smaller strokes on eighth notes.
Play the two up-bow notes gently.

b.

Say "down   slur   down-up   down   up   up"
while clapping steady pulse.

② Go directly from 3rd to 4th finger. See exercise 3 of Minuet No. 2.

③

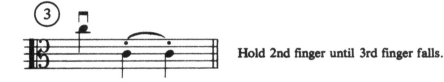

Hold 2nd finger until 3rd finger falls.

Grace note.
Lift and set bow during rests. Listen for a clear grace note.

④

⑤

To find correct finger placement, place 1st finger
silently and hold. Touch 2nd finger to 1st finger.

⑥ **Watch "low-high" 2nd finger.**   **2nd finger lifts as 3rd finger is placed. (Walking fingers)**

First play implied melody with smooth singing quality.

Play melody as Bach wrote it.
Slightly emphasize the melodic notes and relax the accompanying notes.

(The Happy Farmer)

Try this bowing on the C Major (two octave) Scale.

(written)   (played)

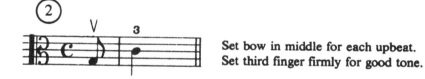

Set bow in middle for each upbeat.
Set third finger firmly for good tone.

Keep 1st finger down when 3rd finger crosses strings.

Listen to correct placement of 1st finger

B♭ touches A

(Gavotte)

Eighth notes should be played staccato. The bow should come to a
full stop on the quarter notes before crossing strings.
Play the grace note on the beat.

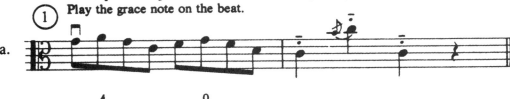

a.

b.   Match clarity of open A string by pressing
firmly with 4th finger.

Use short stroke. Place bow on string; then play, keeping bow on string during rest.

c.

3rd finger is low on G string and high on C string. Use full bows on
quarter notes and upper half or lower half on eighth notes (alternating bowing).
Avoid placing 2nd finger on string when skipping from 1st finger to 3rd finger.

③ Practice holding 2nd finger when placing 3rd finger.

④   First practice slowly with separate bows.

Lift 2   Pull back 2   Place 2

⑤ Developing facility. First practice slowly with separate bows.